little book of

Brandy
Cocktails

little book of

Brandy
Cocktails

hamlyn

First published in 2001 by Hamlyn,

a division of Octopus Publishing Group Limited

2–4 Heron Quays, London E14 4JP

Copyright © 2001 Octopus Publishing Group Ltd

British Library Cataloguing-in-Publication Data

A catalogue record for this book is available from the British Library

ISBN 0 600 60437 3

Printed in China

Notes for American readers

The measure that has been used in the recipes is based on a bar measure,
which is 25 ml (1 fl oz). If preferred, a different volume can be used
providing the proportions are kept constant within a drink and suitable
adjustments are made to spoon measurements, where they occur.

Standard level spoon measurements are used in all recipes.
1 tablespoon = one 15 ml spoon
1 teaspoon = one 5 ml spoon
Imperial and metric measurements have been given in some of the recipes.
Use one set of measurements only.

UK	US
caster sugar	granulated sugar
cocktail cherries	maraschino cherries
cocktail stick	toothpick
double cream	heavy cream
drinking chocolate	presweetened cocoa powder
icing sugar	confectioners' sugar
jug	pitcher
lemon rind	lemon peel or zest
single cream	light cream
soda water	club soda

SAFETY NOTE The Department of Health advises that eggs should not be
consumed raw. This book contains recipes made with raw eggs. It is prudent
for more vulnerable people such as pregnant and nursing mothers, invalids,
the elderly, babies and young children to avoid these recipes.

Contents

Introduction

Although it is better known as an after-dinner drink, savoured from a balloon glass, brandy is also a great mixer.

The name 'brandy' comes from the Dutch word brandewijn meaning 'burnt wine'. It was introduced to northern Europe from France and Spain by Dutch traders in the 16th century. They described it as wine that had been burnt, or boiled, in order to distill it. Brandy is made by distilling wine, fermented juice or mash from any fruit. However, the term is most usually applied to distilled wine made from grapes and the best brandies in the world are made in the great wine-producing areas of France. The history of brandy can be said to be the history of distillation because in the past it was the distillation of wine in crude stills that gave spirits to the world.

Brandy is graded by quality and you should know what to look for when buying a bottle. There are three quality levels: VS (very special) which is also called Three-star and has been aged for at least two-and-a-half years; VO or Reserve VSOP (very superior old pale) which has been aged from four-and-a-half to six-and-a-half years; and XO (extra old) or Extra, the best brandy, that has been aged for at least six-and-a-half years.

Perhaps the most popular brandy in the world is made in the Cognac region of north-western France. It is known for its smoothness and heady scent. Armagnac is much like Cognac but has a richer taste; it is produced in the Armagnac region of south-western France and only brandies produced here can carry the name Armagnac. It is distilled from wines made using the Piquipoul, Colombard, Jurancon and Meslier grape varieties. The black oaks of the region provide the wood for the casks in which the brandy is aged.

The quality of the brandy you choose should depend on the drinks you intend to make. If you are making a punch for a party, choose a relatively inexpensive bottle as the flavour will be masked by the other ingredients. If you are making cocktails of which brandy forms the major part, choose a more expensive bottle as the flavour is more refined.

Brandy comes in many guises and in this book are cocktails made with basic brandy, and those made with other brandy-based drinks including apricot brandy, cherry brandy, Bénédictine and Mandarine Napoléon. Apricot brandy and cherry brandy are both grape brandies that have been flavoured with fruits. The fruits, apricots and cherries, are macerated in the distilled grape wine to produce sweet, fruity brandies that are similar to

liqueurs. Bénédictine is a sweet, golden brandy-based liqueur flavoured with a secret mixture of herbs. It was originally made by Bénédictine monks in Fécamp in Normandy. Mandarine Napoléon is also a brandy-based liqueur that makes a fine cocktail ingredient. It is made by macerating the skins of rare tangerines in a grape brandy and has a punchy tangerine flavour. Whatever ingredients you choose, the recipes in this book show just how versatile brandy can be.

Sugar Syrup

This may be used instead of sugar to sweeten cocktails and give them more body. It can be bought, but is simple to make. Put 4 tablespoons of caster sugar and 4 tablespoons of water in a small pan and stir over a low heat until the sugar has dissolved. Bring to the boil and boil, without stirring, for 1–2 minutes.

7

Variations on a Theme

Tidal Wave

1 measure Mandarine
    Napoléon
4 measures bitter lemon
1 dash lemon juice
6 ice cubes
lemon slice, to decorate

Mix the Mandarine Napoléon,
bitter lemon and lemon juice in
an ice-filled highball glass. Add
a slice of lemon to decorate.

Serves 1

Waterloo

1 measure Mandarine
    Napoléon
4 measures orange juice
6 ice cubes
orange twist, to decorate

**This drink is named after
the famous battle.**

Mix the Mandarine Napoléon
and orange juice in an ice-filled
highball glass. Decorate with a
twist of orange.

Serves 1

Corpse Reviver

3 ice cubes, cracked
2 measures brandy
1 measure calvados
1 measure sweet
    vermouth
apple slice, to decorate

Put the ice, brandy, calvados and sweet vermouth into a cocktail shaker and shake until a frost forms on the outside of the shaker. Strain into a glass and decorate with an apple slice.

Serves 1

Egg Nog

1 measure brandy
1 measure dark rum
1 egg
1 teaspoon sugar syrup
    (see page 7)
3 measures full-fat milk
grated nutmeg, to
    decorate

Shake the brandy, rum, egg and syrup together in a cocktail shaker and strain into a large goblet. Add the milk. Grate some nutmeg on top to decorate.

Serves 1

Brandy Egg Sour

3 ice cubes, cracked

1 egg

1 teaspoon caster sugar

3 dashes lemon juice

1 measure orange
   Curaçao

1 measure brandy

to decorate

orange slice

cocktail cherry

Put the ice, egg, sugar, lemon juice, Curaçao and brandy into a cocktail shaker and shake well. Strain into a tumbler. Decorate with an orange slice speared on a cocktail stick with a cherry. Serve with straws.

Serves 1

15

Brandy Fix

1 teaspoon sugar
1 teaspoon water
2 tablespoons lemon
    juice
½ measure cherry brandy
1 measure brandy
crushed ice
lemon rind spiral, to
    decorate

Dissolve the sugar in the water in a tumbler. Add the remaining ingredients and stir. Decorate the glass with a lemon rind spiral and serve.

Serves 1

French Connection

1 measure brandy
1 measure Amaretto di
    Saronno
4–6 ice cubes

Pour the brandy and Amaretto over ice in an old-fashioned glass.

Serves 1

Shanghai

3 ice cubes, crushed
1 measure brandy
½ measure Curaçao
¼ measure Maraschino
2 dashes Angostura
    bitters

to decorate
lemon rind spiral
cocktail cherry

Put the ice cubes into a cocktail shaker and add the brandy, Curaçao, Maraschino and bitters. Shake to mix. Pour into a cocktail glass and decorate with the lemon rind spiral and a cocktail cherry on a cocktail stick.

Serves 1

18

Brandied Boat

crushed ice
1 measure brandy
2 teaspoons lemon juice
1 teaspoon maraschino
    bitters
1 measure port
lemon rind spiral, to
    decorate

Put the ice into a cocktail shaker. Add the brandy, lemon juice and bitters and shake to mix. Pour into a tumbler and pour over the port. Decorate with a lemon rind spiral.

Serves 1

Brandy Flip

4 ice cubes
1 egg
1½ teaspoons caster
    sugar
2 measures brandy
grated nutmeg, to
    decorate

Put the ice, egg, sugar and
brandy into a cocktail shaker.
Shake well and strain into a
tumbler. Sprinkle a little grated
nutmeg on top.

Serves 1

Variation

For a creamier version,
process the ingredients
in a food processor. Port,
rum, sherry or whisky
can be used in place of
brandy.

Frenchman

2–3 ice cubes, cracked
1 measure brandy
½ measure green
    Chartreuse
3 tablespoons lemon
    juice

Put the ice into a cocktail shaker
and add the brandy, Chartreuse
and lemon juice. Shake to mix
and pour into a cocktail glass.

Serves 1

variations on a theme

23

Leo

2–3 ice cubes, crushed
1 measure brandy
1½ measures orange
    juice
½ measure Amaretto di
    Saronno
soda water
1 teaspoon Campari

**Campari is an Italian
aperitif wine with a strong,
bitter taste and bright red
colour.**

Put the ice into a cocktail shaker.
Add the brandy, orange juice and
Amaretto. Shake well. Strain into
a tall glass and add soda water to
taste, and the Campari.

Serves 1

Brandy Smash

2 mint sprigs
1 teaspoon caster sugar
3 ice cubes, cracked
1 measure brandy
soda water

Crush the mint and sugar together in an old-fashioned glass and rub the mixture around the inside of the glass. Discard the mint. Add the ice cubes and brandy then a splash of soda water.

Serves 1

Variation

To make a Gin Smash, replace the brandy with gin. This drink can also be made with other spirits such as vodka and whisky.

variations on a theme

Angel Face

3 ice cubes, cracked
1 measure gin
1 measure apricot brandy
1 measure calvados
orange rind twist, to
    decorate

Put the ingredients in a cocktail shaker and shake well. Strain into a cocktail glass and add an orange rind twist.

Serves 1

Paradise

3 ice cubes, cracked
1 dash lemon juice
½ measure orange juice
1 measure gin
½ measure apricot brandy
orange and lemon slices,
    to decorate

Put the ingredients in a cocktail shaker and shake well. Strain into a cocktail glass and decorate with orange and lemon slices.

Serves 1

Brandy Fizz

3 ice cubes, cracked
2 tablespoons lemon
    juice
1½ teaspoons caster
    sugar
2 measures brandy
soda water
lemon slice, to decorate

Put the ice, lemon juice, sugar
and brandy into a cocktail
shaker. Shake well, strain into
a tall tumbler and top up with
soda water. Decorate with a
lemon slice.

Serves 1

Variation

To make a Whisky Fizz,
replace the brandy
with whisky.

Singapore Sling

2 ice cubes

2 measures gin

1 measure cherry brandy

1 measure lemon juice

1 measure orange juice

½ measure Cointreau

1–2 dashes Angostura
     bitters

soda water

to decorate

orange slices

cherries

strawberries

Place the ice in a highball glass.
Add the gin, cherry brandy,
lemon and orange juices,
Cointreau and Angostura bitters
and stir well. Top up with soda
water. Decorate with the fruit
speared on a cocktail stick.

Serves 1

Bedtime Bouncer

2 measures brandy
1 measure Cointreau
150 ml (5 fl oz) bitter
    lemon
4–6 ice cubes
lemon rind spiral, to
    decorate

Pour the brandy, Cointreau and bitter lemon into a tumbler, stir well and add the ice. Decorate with the lemon rind spiral and serve with a straw.

Serves 1

Parisien

1 measure brandy
½ measure calvados
1 measure lemon juice
sugar syrup (see page 7)
½ measure Poire William
    (pear liqueur)
fruits, to decorate

Fill a tumbler with crushed ice,
add the spirits, lemon juice and
some sugar syrup to taste. Pour
the Poire William over the top
and decorate with fruits.

Serves 1

Toulon

4–5 ice cubes
1 measure dry vermouth
1 measure Bénédictine
3 measures brandy
orange rind, to decorate

Put the ingredients into a cocktail
shaker and shake well. Strain into
a chilled cocktail glass and
decorate with the orange rind.

Serves 1

Monte Rosa

4–5 ice cubes, cracked
1 tablespoon lime juice
1 measure Cointreau
3 measures brandy

Put the ingredients into a cocktail shaker and shake well. Strain into a chilled cocktail glass.

Serves 1

Capricorn

4 ice cubes, cracked
1 measure Bourbon
    whiskey
½ measure apricot brandy
½ measure lemon juice
2 measures orange juice
orange slice, to decorate

Put half the ice cubes into a cocktail shaker and add the whiskey, apricot brandy, lemon and orange juices. Shake to mix. Put the remaining ice cubes into an old-fashioned glass and strain in the cocktail. Decorate with the orange slice.

Serves 1

Stinger

½ measure white crème
   de menthe
1½ measures brandy
4 ice cubes, cracked
mint sprig, to garnish

Put all the ingredients into a
cocktail shaker and shake well.
Strain into a cocktail glass and
garnish with a mint sprig.

Serves 1

variations on a theme

Party Spirit

Coffee Diablo

Brandy Shrub

Creole Punch

Mulled Ale

Haiti Punch

Loving Cup

Brandy and Lemon Sparkler

Glühwein

Honeysuckle Cup

Tea Punch

Boatman's Cup

Palm Beach Fizz

Glögg

Hot Toddy Supreme

Coffee Diablo

hot black coffee
1 measure brandy
½ measure Cointreau
2 cloves
1 piece of orange rind
1 piece of lemon rind

Make enough hot black coffee
to fill a heatproof glass three-
quarters full. Pour the brandy and
Cointreau into a small saucepan
and add the cloves and orange
and lemon rind. Place the pan
over a low heat. Just before the
mixture comes to the boil, light
it with a long taper and pour the
flaming mixture over the coffee.

Serves 1

Brandy Shrub

grated rind of 2 lemons
juice of 5 lemons
2 bottles brandy
1 bottle sherry
500 g (1 lb) caster sugar

Mix the lemon rind and juice with the brandy in a large bowl or jug. Cover and leave for 3 days. Add the sherry and sugar, stir well to dissolve the sugar, then pour the mixture through a sieve lined with muslin.

Serves 30

Tip

Brandy Shrub keeps well, so any leftover can be poured into a bottle and stored almost indefinitely.

Creole Punch

5 ice cubes, crushed
1½ measures port
½ measure brandy
2 teaspoons lemon juice
lemonade

to decorate
1 orange slice
1 lemon slice
pineapple chunks
cocktail cherries

Put half the ice into a cocktail shaker and add the port, brandy and lemon juice. Shake to mix. Put the remaining ice into a goblet, pour the cocktail over it and top up with lemonade. Decorate with the fruit.

Serves 1

Mulled Ale

1.2 litres (2 pints) brown ale
150 ml (¼ pint) brandy
3 tablespoons brown sugar
6 cloves
1 teaspoon ground ginger
pinch of ground nutmeg
pinch of ground cinnamon
thinly peeled rind and juice of 1 lemon
thinly peeled rind and juice of 1 orange
600 ml (1 pint) water
orange slices, to decorate

Mulls were traditionally mixed at the fireside and heated by plunging a red-hot poker into the pan.

Put all the ingredients into a large saucepan. Bring slowly to the boil, stirring all the time to dissolve the sugar. Turn off the heat and leave to stand for a few minutes. To serve, strain into warmed mugs and float orange slices on top.

Serves 12

Haiti Punch

2 pineapples, peeled and
    cubed
3 lemons, sliced
3 oranges, sliced
300 ml (½ pint) brandy
300 ml (½ pint) Orange
    Nassau liqueur
2 bottles sparkling dry
    white wine

Put the fruit into a large bowl
or jug and pour the brandy and
Orange Nassau over the top.
Cover and chill for several hours.
To serve, pour about 1 measure
of the brandy mixture into a
champagne flute, top up with
sparkling wine and add some
of the pineapple cubes.

Serves 12–15

Tip

The Orange Nassau
liqueur can be replaced
with Cointreau or orange
Curaçao.

46

Loving Cup

8 sugar cubes
2 lemons
½ bottle medium or
    sweet sherry
¼ bottle brandy
1 bottle dry sparkling
    white wine

**This is an ideal drink
to welcome guests on
Christmas day.**

Rub the sugar cubes over the
lemons to absorb the zest. Thinly
peel the lemons and remove as
much of the pith as possible.
Thinly slice the lemons and set
aside. Put the lemon rind, sherry,
brandy and sugar cubes into a
jug and stir until the sugar has
dissolved. Cover and chill in the
refrigerator for about 30 minutes.
To serve, add the wine to the jug
and float the lemon slices on top.

Serves 12

Brandy and Lemon Sparkler

juice of 15 lemons

juice of 4 oranges

625 g (1¼ lb) caster sugar

ice cubes

300 ml (½ pint) orange
    Curaçao

2 measures grenadine

2.25 litres (4 pints)
    brandy

2.25 litres (4 pints)
    sparkling mineral
    water

lemon and orange slices,
    to decorate

Pour the lemon and orange juices into a jug. Add the sugar and stir until dissolved. Place a large quantity of ice in a large punch bowl, add all the ingredients and stir well. Decorate with lemon and orange slices.

Serves 15–20

Glühwein

1 lemon
8 cloves
1 bottle red wine
125 g (4 oz) sugar
2 cinnamon sticks
150 ml (¼ pint) brandy

Spike the lemon with the cloves.
Gently heat the wine, sugar,
cinnamon sticks and lemon
in a saucepan at just below
simmering point for 10 minutes.
Lower the heat and add the
brandy. Warm for 2–3 minutes.
Strain and serve immediately
in warmed glasses or mugs.

Serves 6

Honeysuckle Cup

1 tablespoon clear honey
1 bottle dry white wine
2 tablespoons
    Bénédictine
150 ml (¼ pint) brandy
750 ml (1¼ pints)
    lemonade
1 peach, sliced
fresh raspberries or
    strawberries

Put the honey in a large bowl and gradually stir in the wine. Add the Bénédictine and brandy. Chill for 2 hours. Just before serving, add the lemonade and fruit.

Serves 10–12

Tea Punch

600 ml (1 pint) freshly
    brewed China tea
125 g (4 oz) sugar
juice of 2 lemons
juice of 1 orange
1 cinnamon stick
150 ml (¼ pint) brandy
150 ml (¼ pint) dark rum
3 measures Grand
    Marnier (optional)
about 300 ml (½ pint)
    soda water

to decorate
1 orange, sliced
1 lemon, sliced

Leave the tea to infuse for
10 minutes, then strain into a
large saucepan. Add the sugar
and heat gently until dissolved.
Add the lemon and orange juices,
cinnamon stick, brandy and rum,
and heat gently at just below
simmering point for 5 minutes.
Leave until cold, then chill for 2
hours. Add the Grand Marnier, if
using, and top up with soda
water to taste. To serve, float the
fruit on top.

Serves 8

Boatman's Cup

1 bottle Riesling
500 ml (17 fl oz) still dry cider
4 measures brandy
600 ml (1 pint) fresh orange juice
750 ml (1¼ pints) lemonade
black cherries, halved
1 orange slice
melon balls or cubes
mint sprigs

Mix together the wine, cider, brandy and orange juice. Chill for 2 hours. Just before serving, add the lemonade, fruit and mint.

Serves 14–15

Palm Beach Fizz

1 measure apricot brandy
1 measure orange juice
1 teaspoon Grand
    Marnier
Champagne or sparkling
    dry white wine

Put the apricot brandy, orange juice and Grand Marnier in a Champagne flute or cocktail glass and stir well. Top up with Champagne or sparkling wine.

Serves 1

Variation

Use peach brandy instead of apricot brandy and Galliano instead of Grand Marnier.

Glögg

75 g (3 oz) sugar
1 bottle brandy
12 cloves
pinch of ground
    cinnamon
pinch of grated nutmeg
50 g (2 oz) large raisins
50 g (2 oz) unsalted
    blanched almonds
1 litre (1¾ pints) medium
    sweet sherry

Dissolve the sugar in the brandy over a gentle heat in a saucepan. Add the cloves, cinnamon, nutmeg, raisins and almonds, and heat at just below simmering point for 10 minutes. Heat the sherry separately to just below simmering point. Ignite the brandy mixture and pour in the sherry. Serve immediately in warmed glasses or mugs.

Serves 8–10

Hot Toddy Supreme

2 measures Stone's
ginger wine
1 measure brandy
1 tablespoon double
cream
1 cinnamon stick
½ teaspoon grated
orange rind

Gently heat the ginger wine and brandy in a saucepan to just below boiling point. Pour into a warmed cup or glass and gently pour the cream over the back of a spoon on to the surface. Add the cinnamon stick and sprinkle the orange rind over the top.

Serves 1

Surprise Treats

Apricot Sour	Frozen Apricot Sour
Alexander	Harlequin
Penguin	Tropical Tonic
Pousse Café	American Beauty
Zombie	Bobby Jones
Frozen Alexander	Pink Treasure
Baltimore Egg Nog	Banana Bliss
Cherry Blossom	Jolly Roger
Frozen Mandarine Sour	Secret Smile
Morning	American Rose
Honeymoon	East India
Royal Wedding	Monte Carlo Sling
Burnt Orange	Fifth Avenue

Apricot Sour

2 ice cubes, cracked
1 measure apricot brandy
1 measure lemon juice
1 dash Angostura bitters
1 dash egg white
1 apricot wedge,
    chopped

to decorate
lemon slice
cocktail cherry

Put the ingredients into a cocktail shaker and shake vigorously. Strain into a tumbler and decorate with a lemon slice and a cocktail cherry speared on a cocktail stick.

Serves 1

Alexander

3 ice cubes, cracked
1 measure brandy
1 measure brown crème
    de cacao
1 measure single cream
cocoa powder

Put all the ingredients into a cocktail shaker and shake well. Strain into a cocktail glass and sprinkle the top with cocoa powder.

Serves 1

Penguin

1 measure brandy
½ measure Cointreau
1 measure lemon juice
1 measure orange juice
1 dash grenadine
6 ice cubes

to decorate
¼ orange slice
¼ lemon slice

Pour the brandy, Cointreau, lemon juice, orange juice and grenadine into a mixing glass and stir well. Fill a tall glass with ice. Pour the drink into the glass and decorate with the orange and lemon slices placed on the rim of the glass. Serve with 2 long straws.

Serves 1

Pousse Café

½ measure Grenadine
½ measure Maraschino
½ measure crème de
    violette
½ measure Chartreuse
½ measure brandy

Maraschino is a colourless liqueur from Italy made with sour maraschino cherries and their crushed kernels.

Carefully pour each of the ingredients in turn into a tumbler or highball glass to form separate layers. The effect should be like a rainbow of distinct colours.

Serves 1

surprise treats

Zombie

3 ice cubes, cracked
1 measure dark rum
1 measure white rum
½ measure apricot brandy
2 measures pineapple
    juice
1 tablespoon lime juice
2 teaspoons caster sugar

to decorate
cocktail cherry
pineapple wedge
mint sprig
caster sugar (optional)

This is reputed to be the strongest of all cocktails, so take care!

Place a hurricane glass, or tall glass, in the freezer until the outside becomes frosted. Put the ice into a cocktail shaker, add the rums, apricot brandy, fruit juices and sugar. Shake to mix. Pour into the glass without straining. To decorate, spear the cherry and pineapple on to a cocktail stick and place across the top of the glass. Add the mint sprig and sprinkle powdered sugar over the drink, if liked. Serve with straws.

Serves 1

Frozen Alexander

1 measure brandy
1 measure brown crème
   de cacao
1 scoop vanilla ice-cream
4–6 ice cubes, cracked
chocolate powder, to
   decorate

Place the ingredients in a food processor and process together. Pour into an ice-filled glass and sprinkle with chocolate powder.

Serves 1

Baltimore Egg Nog

1 egg
1½ teaspoons sugar
½ measure brandy
½ measure dark rum
½ measure Madeira
200 ml (7 fl oz) milk
grated nutmeg, to
   decorate

Put all the ingredients into a cocktail shaker and shake well. Strain into a tall glass and sprinkle the top with nutmeg.

Serves 1

Cherry Blossom

1 measure cherry brandy
caster sugar
4 ice cubes, cracked
1 measure cognac
1 dash lemon juice
1 dash Cointreau
1 dash grenadine

Frost the rim of a cocktail glass
with a little of the cherry brandy
and the caster sugar. Put the
remaining cherry brandy and the
rest of the ingredients into a
cocktail shaker and shake well.
Strain into the frosted glass.

Serves 1

Frozen Mandarine Sour

2 measures Mandarine
   Napolèon
1 measure lemon juice
1 scoop vanilla ice-cream
4 ice cubes, cracked

Place the ingredients in a food processor and process together. Pour into an ice-filled glass.

Serves 1

Morning

4–5 ice cubes
3 dashes Angostura
    bitters
5 dashes Pernod
½ teaspoon grenadine
½ teaspoon dry vermouth
1 measure Curaçao
3 measures brandy
cocktail cherries, to
    decorate

Put the ice cubes into a cocktail shaker. Shake the bitters over the ice, and add the Pernod. Pour in the grenadine, vermouth, Curaçao and brandy, shake well then strain into a chilled cocktail glass and decorate with cocktail cherries on a cocktail stick.

Serves 1

Honeymoon

2–3 ice cubes, cracked
1 measure Calvados
½ measure Bénédictine
2 teaspoons orange juice
1 teaspoon Cointreau

Put the ice cubes into a cocktail shaker and add the Calvados. Bénédictine and orange juice. Shake to mix. Strain into a cocktail glass. Pour the Cointreau on to the surface but do not stir.

Serves 1

Royal Wedding

2–3 ice cubes, cracked
1 measure brandy
½ measure peach brandy
½ measure kirsch
2 measures orange juice
soda water

To decorate
peach slices
orange slices
cocktail cherries

Put the ice cubes into a cocktail shaker. Add the brandy, peach brandy, kirsch and orange juice and shake to mix. Pour into a tall glass and top up with soda water. Decorate with the peach slices, orange slices and cherries.

Serves 1

Burnt Orange

4–5 ice cubes
3 drops orange bitters or
	Angostura bitters
juice of ½ orange
3 measures brandy
orange slice, to decorate

Put the ice cubes into a cocktail shaker. Shake the bitters over the ice, add the orange juice and brandy and shake vigorously. Strain into a chilled cocktail glass and serve decorated with an orange slice.

Serves 1

Frozen Apricot Sour

2 measures apricot
	brandy
1 measure lemon juice
1 scoop vanilla ice-cream
4 ice cubes, cracked

Place the ingredients in a food processor and process together. Pour into an ice-filled glass.

Serves 1

Harlequin

lightly beaten egg white
caster sugar
1 measure kirsch
1 measure apricot brandy
2 measures orange juice
soda water

to decorate
1 orange slice
2 cocktail cherries

Dip the rim of a tumbler in the
lightly beaten egg white, then in
caster sugar. Place the kirsch,
apricot brandy and orange juice
in a cocktail shaker. Shake lightly.
Strain into the glass and top up
with soda water. Decorate with
the orange slice and cherries.

Serves 1

Tropical Tonic

2 measures Malibu
1 measure Mandarine
    Napolèon
5 ice cubes, cracked
5 measures ginger ale

Combine the Malibu and the
Mandarine Napolèon in an ice-
filled highball glass. Top up the
glass with ginger ale.

Serves 1

American Beauty

4–5 ice cubes
1 measure brandy
1 measure dry vermouth
1 measure orange juice
1 measure grenadine
1 dash crème de menthe
ruby port

to decorate
cocktail cherry
orange slice
mint sprig

Put the ice cubes into a cocktail shaker and pour in the brandy, vermouth, orange juice, grenadine and crème de menthe. Shake well and strain into a cocktail glass. Tilt the glass and gently pour in a little ruby port so that it floats on top. Decorate with a cocktail cherry, orange slice and mint sprig on a cocktail stick.

Serves 1

Bobby Jones

4–5 ice cubes
juice of 1 lemon
½ teaspoon grenadine
1 measure crème de
    cacao
3 measures brandy

This cocktail is named after Bobby Jones, the American golfer whose heyday was in the 1920s and '30s. He is regarded as the greatest amateur player of all time.

Put the ice cubes into a cocktail shaker. Pour the lemon juice, grenadine, crème de cacao and brandy over the ice and shake until a frost forms on the outside of the shaker. Strain into a tumbler and serve with a straw.

Serves 1

Pink Treasure

2 ice cubes, cracked
1 measure white rum
1 measure cherry brandy
bitter lemon or soda
 water (optional)
lemon rind spiral, to
 decorate

Put the ice cubes, rum and cherry
brandy into a small glass. Add a
splash of bitter lemon or soda
water, if using. Decorate with the
lemon rind spiral.

Serves 1

Banana Bliss

4–5 ice cubes
1 measure brandy
1 measure crème de
    banane
1 measure Cointreau

to decorate
banana slice
lemon juice

Put the ice cubes into a mixing glass and pour in the brandy, crème de banane and Cointreau. Stir with a spoon then strain into a cocktail glass. Dip the banana slice into lemon juice to prevent it discolouring then attach it to the rim of the glass.

Serves 1

Jolly Roger

5 ice cubes, cracked
1 measure dark rum
1 measure Galliano
½ measure apricot brandy
3 measures orange juice

to decorate
apricot slice
orange slice
lemon slice

Put half of the ice cubes into a cocktail shaker. Add the rum, Galliano, apricot brandy and orange juice. Shake to mix. Put the remaining ice into a tall glass and strain the cocktail over it. Decorate with the fruit slices.

Serves 1

Tip

Galliano is a golden liqueur flavoured with liquorice and aniseed, produced in Milan, Italy.

Secret Smile

lightly beaten egg white
caster sugar
1 measure orange juice
½ measure Galliano
½ measure brandy
Champagne or sparkling
    dry white wine
orange rind spiral, to
    decorate

Dip the rim of a Champagne flute
or tall glass in the beaten egg
white, then in the caster sugar
to frost. Pour in the orange juice,
Galliano and brandy and top up
with the Champagne or sparkling
wine. Decorate the rim of the
glass with the orange rind spiral.

Serves 1

American Rose

4–5 ice cubes
1 measure brandy
1 dash Pernod
1 dash grenadine
½ ripe peach, skinned,
    stoned and roughly
    chopped
crushed ice
Champagne
peach or mango slices,
    to decorate

Put the ice cubes into a cocktail shaker. Pour in the brandy, Pernod and grenadine and add the peach. Fill a cocktail glass with crushed ice. Shake the mixture well then strain into the glass. Top up with Champagne just before serving and add peach or mango slices to decorate.

Serves 1

East India

4–5 ice cubes
3 drops Angostura bitters
½ measure pineapple
    juice
½ measure blue Curaçao
2 measures brandy
orange rind spiral, to
    decorate

Put the ice cubes into a mixing glass. Shake the bitters over the ice and add the pineapple juice, Curaçao and brandy. Stir until frothy, then strain into a chilled cocktail glass. Decorate with an orange rind spiral.

Serves 1

Monte Carlo Sling

5 seedless grapes
crushed ice
1 measure brandy
½ measure peach liqueur
1 measure ruby port
1 measure lemon juice
½ measure orange juice
dash orange bitters
2 measures Champagne
grapes, to decorate

Put the 5 grapes into a tall glass and crush them, then fill the glass with crushed ice. Put all the rest of the ingredients except for the Champagne into a cocktail shaker and add more ice. Shake, then strain into the glass. Top with the Champagne, decorate the glass with the grapes and serve.

Serves 1

Fifth Avenue

1 measure brown crème
    de cacao
1 measure apricot brandy
1 measure cream

Pour the ingredients carefully in the order given into a straight-sided liqueur glass so that each ingredient floats on the preceding one.

Serves 1

INDEX

NEW PHOTOGRAPHY
by William Reavell
Cocktails styled by
Andrew Fitz-Maurice at
High Holborn, 95–96 High
Holborn, London WC1V 6LF

ACKNOWLEDGEMENTS
IN SOURCE ORDER
Little Book of Brandy
Cocktails

**Octopus Publishing
Group Limited/** Neil Mersh
67/ Sandra Lane 45, 48, 51,
74/ William Reavell front
cover, back cover, 2, 3, 5,
6–7 background, 8, 11, 13,
15, 17, 19, 21, 24, 27, 28,
31, 32, 36, 38, 41, 47, 55,
56, 60, 62, 69, 73, 77, 78,
80, 85, 89, 90, 93, 95/ Ian
Wallace 83